What Was It Like?™
JACKIE ROBINSON

by Lawrence Weinberg
illustrated by George Ford

Longmeadow Press

Published by Longmeadow Press
201 High Ridge Road, Stamford, CT 06904

ANGEL
ENTERTAINMENT INC

T here is an invisible wall between white and black Americans. It is a big, thick wall that was built long ago, when black people were slaves to white people. Even after the Emancipation Proclamation freed the slaves in 1863, the wall still stood. It had crumbled slightly, but it was still there. The cement that holds this wall together is racism. Racism is the belief that one race of people is better than another. I like to think that I helped to break down a little bit of that wall during my lifetime. I chipped away at it with a baseball bat and ball. My name is Jackie Robinson and this is the story of my life.

I was the first black baseball player in the major leagues. I fought racism every day of my life in many other, less well-known ways, too.

I was born in a cabin in Cairo, Georgia, on January 31, 1919. The cabin had been part of a slave plantation before the Civil War. After the war, the white man who owned all the land separated his land into small parcels, which were farmed by people like my father. These farmers were called sharecroppers because they had to share whatever they

grew with the man who owned the land.

Life was hard on that farm. We never had enough crops left to sell after giving a share to the white owner, and just barely enough to feed ourselves. The owner paid my father a salary, but it was not enough to support a family of seven. My father left the plantation to look for work somewhere else. He said he would send for us as soon as he could. We never heard from him again. When the owner found out that there was no man working our parcel, he kicked my mother off his property.

If Mallie Robinson, my mother, was frightened about the future, she didn't show it to her children. She put her faith in God, and in her own determination to take care of her family. She was a strong woman. Her grandfather had been a slave and now she was setting out on her own with five small children to build a new life. She had an older brother, Frank, who'd settled on the other side of the country in California after World War I. He sent a letter inviting us to come out and stay with him until she could find work.

My mother knew that schools in California where Frank lived were not segregated. This meant that white and black children could go to the same public schools instead of to separate ones as they did in Georgia and the rest of the southern states.

We left Georgia and took bus after bus for almost a week, traveling day and night, before we reached the city of Pasadena in California. My mother found some white women who would give her work cleaning house. Soon, she was working steadily, and my brothers and sister worked after school. I was a problem, though. I was too small to stay at home alone, but too young for school. But who was going to watch a small boy like me when she couldn't afford to hire anyone?

There's an old saying that goes, "Where there's a will, there's a way." My mother always had the will. Every day, my sister Willa Mae took me with her and put me in a sandbox in the schoolyard playground. The teacher let her sit by the window where she could watch me from her classroom. I played by myself all day long. I didn't mind it at all—until the first time it started to rain. Willa Mae wouldn't sit still until her teacher allowed her to run outside and bring me into the building.

In those days, we didn't get to see too much of our mother. She was up before daylight to go to work, and she came home so late, it was almost time for bed. I still don't know how she managed to do it, but she scraped enough money together to make the first payment on a house on Pepper Street. We lived in that house for twenty-four years.

Even with my mother's salary, the little money the other children made, rent from boarders and the small amount we would sometimes get from welfare, there was never enough to go around. But there were always kind people ready to help us when we needed it. The bakery down the street would save their extra bread, and one of us kids would run down there at the end of the day to pick it up at no charge. The milkman would leave any extra bottles on our stoop after his rounds were over.

Not everyone was nice, though. We were the only black people living on the block. Some of the owners of the other houses were angry with us for daring to live in their neighborhood. These people wanted us to move out. They thought if they harassed us enough, we would *want* to leave. The police were called to arrest my brother Edgar because his roller skates were making too much noise on the sidewalk. A woman across the street would slam her door

every time we came outside.

Some of our neighbors were more violent. I was about eight years old when a little white girl who lived across the street saw me sweeping the sidewalk in front of my house. "Nigger, nigger, nigger," she started shouting at me. When I called her a name back, she picked up stones and began throwing them at me. Then, her father came out, but not to break up the fight. He picked up stones, too. He screamed that we didn't belong on this block, and tried to hit me with his stones. This was my street as well as his, so I fought back. Finally, the man's wife dragged him into his house.

I loved sports even then—any sport. I would come home from school and go right out and play ball with my brothers and their friends. I think that playing with all those kids made me faster because they were so much bigger than I was. I fell in love with baseball when I was eight years old. I used to practice in front of my house, hitting a ball my mother had made for me out of old woolen socks with a stick for a bat. In a way, I became a professional ball player when I was still in grade school. The kids in school used to offer me parts of their lunches, or even money, to play on their teams. I would rush right home after school with the extra food or money to give to my mother and sister and brothers. I wanted to help out, too.

In a few years, things began to get a little better on Pepper Street. A few more black families moved into the area, as well as some Mexicans and Asians. I got together with some of the boys, and we began to call ourselves the Pepper Street Gang. We weren't out to cause trouble. We just wanted what other boys wanted. We weren't allowed to go to the movies because the only theater in town didn't have a section for the "colored." Only whites could go. And in the summer, we were only allowed to use the city pool once a week. But white people could swim whenever they wanted.

We went to the reservoir, instead, where no one was allowed to swim, and got into trouble with the police. The older we grew, the wilder the Pepper Street Gang became. Hardly a week went by when we didn't have to report to Captain Morgan of the Police Department's Youth Division. It was clear to everyone except us that we were only going to get into deeper trouble as we got older.

Fortunately, someone cared enough to try to set us straight. There was a black automobile

mechanic named Carl Anderson working in our neighborhood. He'd been watching us for a long time, and one day he took us aside. "Boys," he said, "most of you only pull that kind of stuff because you want what everyone else has. You won't get it by breaking the law, though. That will just make things worse. Put your energy into something positive, and maybe you can change things."

Mr. Anderson really made me think. I broke away from that gang and turned to sports with more energy than ever before. I loved to win. I still loved baseball, but football was where I could really let off steam. I didn't weigh very much compared to some of the other players, but I was fast and wouldn't let anyone stop me from scoring a touchdown.

Before I left high school, I'd earned varsity letters for excellence in football, baseball, basketball and track. After I graduated, I enrolled in Pasadena Junior College. My brother Mack was already well-known there, because he had finished second to Jesse Owens in the two hundred meter dash during the 1936 Olympics. He had set all his college records there before he

went to the Olympics. I hoped that I would do the same justice to the Robinson name.

I joined the football, baseball, basketball and track teams. I played football in the fall, and basketball in the winter. I had a problem in the spring because I was both running track and playing baseball. It was difficult when I had a track meet in the morning and a baseball game in the afternoon—forty miles away! I would run my races, and then run right into a waiting car to drive to the game.

My name began to show up in the newspapers in Pasadena. They said I was a terrific all-around athlete. I was quarterback on the football team, shortstop on the baseball team, a starting player on the basketball team, as well as running track. I must have been doing something right, because I set an American junior college record in the broad jump—a record my brother Mack had held. Our teams were winning championships, too. I was voted the most valuable junior college player in Southern California.

Coaches from famous colleges must have been reading those newspapers, because many of them wanted me to come and play for them. I

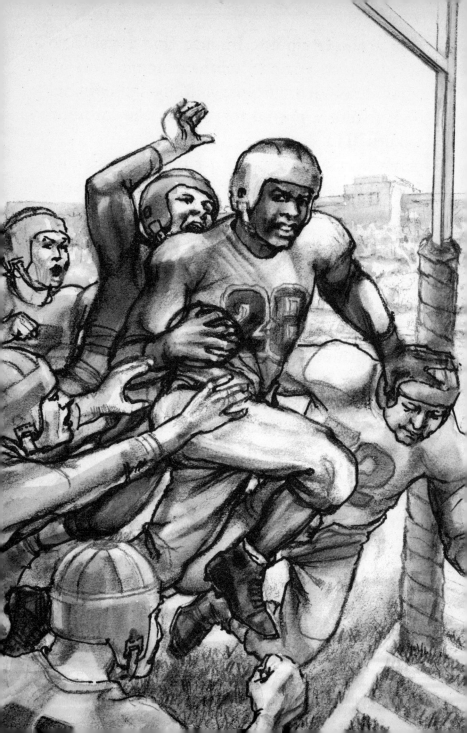

wanted to stay close to my family, though. My brother Frank came to most of my games and meets. He helped me believe in myself. I chose to go to UCLA, the University of California at Los Angeles.

A few weeks after I enrolled at UCLA, Frank was killed in a motorcycle accident. I threw myself into sports even more. In my first year at UCLA, I went out for the football, basketball, track and baseball teams. By the end of the year, I was the first person in the history of the school to win varsity letters in all four of them.

Football was the biggest college game in those days. I was lucky enough to be on UCLA's first undefeated team. I played a great game against Stanford that year, the best team in the country. We were in the last half and behind by a score of seven to fourteen. Their quarterback threw a pass and I intercepted it and ran it back sixty-five yards. On the next play, we scored. My punt tied the game. The UCLA fans and the sportscasters went wild. They were saying, "Jackie Robinson is the greatest college athlete of all time!" I don't know how true that was, but it was nice to hear it. I also won the title of All-American.

I fell in love with another student, Rachel Isum. I asked Rae to go to a dance with me. I think she began to like me after that dance.

I worked part-time jobs, and I tried to help my mother out as much as I could. But, I didn't see what an education could do for me, a black man. My brother Mack had been a college graduate and had won an Olympic medal, and he still couldn't get a decent job. My mother wanted me to stay and get my diploma. Looking back, she was probably right. At that moment, though, I just didn't think it was going to help.

I took a job working with poor children in a youth camp, run by the government. I loved helping kids who were growing up with the same problems I had had.

Everything changed on December 7, 1941. Japanese airmen attacked an American naval base at Pearl Harbor in the Pacific Ocean. We were at war now with Japan and Germany. Money was needed to build up an army, navy and air force. There was no money left to help the underprivileged kids I had been working with.

I received a letter telling me to report for duty to the United States Army. I was sent to Fort Riley, a basic training camp in Kansas. Fort Riley had an officers training program and I applied. I was qualified for it, even though I did not complete my last year at UCLA. I got no reply, and neither did any of the other black soldiers who applied. I went to see Joe Louis, the heavyweight boxing champion of the world, who was stationed at Fort Riley. Joe knew some important people in the government, including the President of the United States, Franklin D. Roosevelt. He must have spoken to the right people, because it wasn't long before I was in Officers Candidates School, along with the other black soldiers. I got my second lieutenant's bars in 1943.

It was at about this time that I began to really fight against racism. The army was a great place to start. Black soldiers were still kept in separate units. How could blacks fight for their country and give up their lives, if their country did not think they were good enough to fight next to white soldiers? Even off duty units were still separated by color. At the Post Exchange restaurant white soldiers could walk in, sit down wherever they pleased and order. There

were only a few places set aside for black soldiers, though, so that they had to wait for a seat to open up, no matter how many seats in the white section were empty. I'd gotten into an argument with a major about this, but in the end, we got more seats.

I was put in charge of running a tank platoon at another base, in Texas. My commanding officer praised the work I did in getting my platoon ready to go overseas. One day before I left, I got on a bus and sat down in a seat in the middle section (in those days blacks were only allowed to sit in the back of the bus) with a black woman. The white bus driver ordered me to leave my seat and get to the back of the bus. I knew that the government had passed a law stating that a bus that traveled on government property could not be segregated. We were on a military base.

I wouldn't move and the driver was furious. He jumped off the bus and called some military policemen over to take me off the bus. I was charged with being drunk and put on trial for "conduct unbecoming an officer." I had learned that an athlete who smoked and drank lost a lot of his edge every time he went out on the playing field. I loved to win too much to give up any edge I might have had. I was found not guilty, but by that time the troops I'd trained had gone overseas without me.

I stayed on at the base while the fighting raged in Europe. I realized that the army life was not for me, and began to wonder what I'd do when I left. I was thinking about this one day while walking across the base. I heard the crack of a bat from a nearby playing field. When I looked around, there was a baseball flying at me. I caught it and threw it back to the black soldier who was practicing his hitting. We played a bit, and then got to talking.

He told me that before the war he'd played ball for an all-black team called the Kansas City Monarchs. He told me to write to them and ask for a tryout. I took his advice and received a letter asking me to come to the team's spring training camp in Houston, Texas.

It was April of 1945. There was even more segregation in baseball than there had been in the army. In baseball, blacks and whites couldn't even play in the same league.

However, in America during the baseball season, there was only one kind of "organized" baseball—white baseball. No black player ever even considered the possibility of playing in organized baseball. The black league had its own particular kind of excitement. We relied on tricky pitches and fancy base stealing to win games. The fans loved the way I had of driving the other team's pitcher crazy once I was on base. A player is allowed to steal bases after he has gotten a hit or a walk. The runner must get to the next base before the pitcher or the catcher gets the ball to the baseman to tag the runner out. I'd take a long lead off of the base, pretending I was just about to run for the next one. Then suddenly, I'd fade back as if I'd changed my mind. As soon as the pitcher started his windup for another pitch, I'd take another long lead off the base. Sometimes I got the pitcher so mixed up that he practically dropped the ball—then I was off running to second base, or third base or even stealing home! Stealing home was the hardest because the pitcher threw the ball to the catcher anyway when he pitched, and the catcher could tag you out very easily. Runners almost never stole home in organized baseball. I guess you could say that stealing home was almost my trademark in baseball.

Playing baseball for the Kansas City Monarchs was great, except for the traveling. We had a team bus, but we had to drive all over the country. It was especially hard in the South. For

weeks at a time we would live in the team bus, eating take-out food because restaurants wouldn't allow us to sit inside and eat, and sleeping in the bus because most hotels would not allow blacks to rent rooms.

Many players tried not to let it bother them. They really loved baseball, and were glad of any opportunity to play it. We didn't get nearly as much money as white players nor as much attention. We had men who could hit like Babe Ruth, but the newspaper reporters didn't come to see them play, and the sportscasters on the radio didn't mention their names. Even the black fans only talked about white baseball stars.

One day the Monarchs were playing in Chicago, Illinois. A man came over to speak to me after the game. "My name is Clyde Sukeforth," he said. "I work for the Brooklyn Dodgers. I'm scouting for a new black league being formed."

Then he asked me to fly back to New York with him to see the head of the Dodgers, Branch Rickey.

I did not think that the Dodgers would send a man out to Chicago and fly me all the way back to New York just to start another black league. I did not dare think that maybe they were scouting for organized, white baseball.

Rickey had been thinking about bringing a black player into white baseball. He'd hated racism all his life, and decided that now the time was right to do something about it in baseball. He knew that there would be trouble— with the other owners, the other players and the fans. He told Clyde to find, "one very good ball player. He has got to be more than a ball player. He is going to have to take a lot of abuse. He may even be in danger. I need somebody who can take all that and still play great baseball. He also has to have a good character. I want a man whom the fans and papers are going to have to respect whether they like it at first or not! I don't want the newspapers to find out what's going on. If people want to know what's going on, tell them that I'm thinking about starting a new black league."

I found out Branch Rickey's plans for me when I met him in New York. He leaned across his desk and said, "Robinson, I'm interested in bringing you into the Brooklyn organization. Maybe Montreal to begin with."

The Montreal Royals was an all-white club owned by the Dodgers. It was called a "farm team" because Rickey used it to raise a crop of baseball players who could later move up into the major leagues. If I proved myself a good player in organized baseball's minor leagues, then I would be moved up to the major leagues, and the Brooklyn Dodgers.

Rickey turned to Clyde, "Can he do it?"

"He can run, he can field and he can hit," said Clyde.

"Yes, but has he got the guts?"

I didn't like them talking about me like I wasn't even there. "If you know anything about me at all, you know that I have!"

After I'd calmed down, Rickey said that he knew I wasn't afraid to fight back, but that would not help me. The angry fans who would be calling me dirty names, and the resentful ball players would be counting on me to fight back. If black fans came to my aid, I would be blamed by the sportswriters for starting riots.

That would give these people the excuse they needed to say, "Here's the proof that the races can't be mixed in baseball!"

I understood all of this, but I did not know if I could be like that. All my life I had fought back. "Mr. Rickey," I demanded, "are you looking for a Negro who is afraid to fight back?"

The old man boomed right back at me, "I'm looking for a ballplayer with courage enough *not* to fight back!"

I had gone to that meeting thinking that maybe I would get a shot at organized baseball. I knew now that I would be doing a lot more than playing baseball. I would be fighting racism just by playing. I knew that the rougher things got, the harder I would have to play. Millions of white people would be watching my every move, and millions of black people would be counting on me. I had no intention of letting anyone down.

Once the press heard about Branch's "noble experiment," sportswriters and broadcasters couldn't stop talking about my chances of succeeding. Some said that black players just couldn't be as good as whites. For one thing, they felt that, "Blacks just didn't have the same kind of will to win that white people did." From one end of the country to the other, you could read and hear predictions that I would never be allowed the chance to put on a Brooklyn Dodger uniform.

I believed in myself, though, and so did the girl I loved. Two weeks after Rae and I got married, we headed for Daytona Beach, Florida, where Montreal was beginning spring training.

We were bumped from two flights on our way to Florida, and ended up taking a Greyhound bus. We finally reached Daytona Beach and found out that we would not be able to stay in the hotel with the other players. It was for whites only. Instead, we had to stay with a friendly local black family.

If I didn't have enough problems getting to Florida and staying there, I was having problems playing baseball. I knew how much my playing meant and I was trying too hard. I strained my arm. My hitting was terrible.

Soon the team began traveling around Florida to play other clubs. I had trouble almost right away. In the middle of one of our first games, a man wearing a sheriff's badge walked out on the field and grabbed me.

"You get off this field right now," he shouted at me, "or I'll throw you in jail. We ain't having none of your kind playing on the same field with white boys."

That was just the beginning. The sheriffs and mayors of other towns where we were scheduled to play cancelled our games before we even got there. We'd pull up in front of a stadium only to find everybody gone and a padlock on the gate. Branch told us to just play games at our training camp.

I became more and more nervous as the official baseball season approached. Opening day was in Jersey City, New Jersey. More than 35,000 people jammed the stadium. Thousands of them were black people and most of them had come to see *me* play. I was the second man to bat. The first pitch was a strike. The one after that was a ball. When the next pitch came whizzing past me, I felt as if my bat weighed one hundred pounds. I couldn't connect it with the ball. It was strike two. I tried to swing at the next pitch, but I couldn't move my arm. Luckily the pitch was a ball. I stepped out of the batter's box. I bent over and rubbed some dirt on my hands. The pitch came in. I swung and connected. It was a weak hit. The ball just rolled to the shortstop. He picked it up and threw it to the first baseman and I was out.

"At least I've hit the ball!" I told myself.

A few innings later, I was at bat again. This time I was ready. I took my time waiting for the right pitch. The call was a full count before I saw it. A full count is three balls and two strikes. I swung at the next pitch with all my might. The ball soared three hundred and forty feet away from me for a home run! As I ran around the bases, black and white people alike, stood up and cheered for me. When I crossed home plate, my teammates ran over to congratulate me.

I was back in the swing of it now. By the time the game ended in victory for our team, I had four hits and two stolen bases. Now I felt like I was holding up to some of my responsibilities as a black baseball player.

The Royals' home city was in Montreal, Canada. It was a wonderful experience playing baseball in Canada. There was no wall there between whites and blacks. Canadians didn't believe in racial segregation the way Americans did.

The Montreal fans appreciated me for what I could do for their baseball team. They didn't seem to care that I was black. The Montreal fans liked my playing style, how I stole bases and made the game exciting.

We were winning game after game and I had the best batting average in the International League. I was still nervous though, with all the responsibility I felt. It became so bad after a while that I couldn't sleep well, and often couldn't eat. A doctor told me that I could have a nervous breakdown.

I couldn't take a vacation because the World Series of minor leagues was approaching quickly. We were playing the Louisville Colonels for the championship. We played the first three games of the series in the Colonels' stadium down south in Kentucky. Many blacks who wanted to see me play were barred entrance there. The white fans jeered and booed like crazy. I wasn't prepared for such hatred, and neither were my teammates. We lost our edge, some of our competitiveness, as well as the first two games. The first team to win four games in the series would win the championship. We managed to win the next game before heading back to Montreal.

We thought we would win by a lot in the fourth game in Canada. By the final inning, it looked as if we had thought wrong. The Colonels were leading five runs to four. Then things started to heat up in the last inning. I led off by reaching first base. Two other players also got on base. Now, the bases were loaded. I was on third base. It was time to show the Colonels what a little black-league-style base running was all about.

I wasn't taking a long lead off third base, so the pitcher didn't expect me to attempt to steal home. As soon as he went into his wind-up, I shot towards home plate. Then, I stopped, spun around and raced back to third base before the third baseman could tag me out. The pitcher was so rattled that the next time I took off towards home, he threw the ball a little wildly. The catcher was able to stop the ball with his mitt, but he couldn't hold on to it and it rolled behind him. I slid into home base for the tying run. The next time I came to bat, I drove in the winning run.

The series was even now, two games to two, and we were ready to win the next two. Our fans cheered us on to those wins, and the Minor League Championship of the world. The people of Montreal lifted me onto their shoulders and carried me around the field, and then through the streets to my hotel.

I had proved myself on the Dodger farm team, but Branch wasn't ready to bring me up to the

majors yet. I went to spring training with Montreal again, and switched my position from shortstop to first baseman. I didn't really like my new position at first. The Dodgers had a great shortstop, though, Pee Wee Reese. Branch had us play some practice games against the Dodgers. It was important that the Dodgers see that I was a good baseball player because there were some players who told Branch they would quit if I ever joined the major leagues.

During the last exhibition game before the official 1947 baseball season opened, Branch made his announcement. He walked up to the press box at Ebbets Field, the Dodgers' stadium in Brooklyn, and handed a note to each reporter covering the game. Sportswriters were climbing all over each other to get to the telephones with the news. "Jackie Robinson is going to play for the Brooklyn Dodgers," they yelled.

I was really nervous now that I was in the national spotlight in the major leagues. And New York City was a city where any man, black or white, was going to have to show the fans that he was worth the number on the back of his jersey. My number was forty-two. The opening day crowd at Ebbets Field was jammed into the bleachers. I didn't win their hearts that day. I was tagged out at first after I hit a ground ball, called out after I hit a fly ball and someone caught it and smacked my last hit into a double play that got another Dodger player out as well as myself.

The next game I managed to get a hit by bunting with the center of my bat, and running as fast as I could to first base.

The third game, the Dodgers traveled to the Polo Grounds to play our arch rivals, the New York Giants. I hit my first home run in the major leagues. I was finally beginning to play baseball.

Even though my hitting was improving, the playing conditions were not. The Philadelphia Phillies were one of the worst teams for me to play. Their manager hated blacks. He ordered his players to insult me whenever they could. Some of the Dodger players, though, actually began grumbling about the unfairness of the Phillies treatment of me. Our second baseman called for a time out, and walked over to me. He was one of the Dodgers who had threatened to quit if I played for them. Up until that moment, he would not even stay in the same dugout with me, but now, he said, "Don't let those bums get you down." And then he gave me a tip on how to field for the batter who was up. I finally began to feel as if I were part of a *team*.

In the eighth inning, I came to bat. We had been scoreless until then, but now I hit the ball into center field for a single. I took off from first. I stole second safely! Then I stole third! The next batter hit a single and I ran home. We won that game against the Phillies, one to zero. It was a sweet victory for me.

The Phillies weren't the only team that caused me problems. The Cardinals said they would go on strike rather than play me in a game. I had even heard that some of my own team members had suggested the idea to them. Luckily, the Baseball Commissioner told the Cardinals that they would be thrown out of the league if they held a strike.

It wasn't only other baseball players and teams that were giving me problems. I started

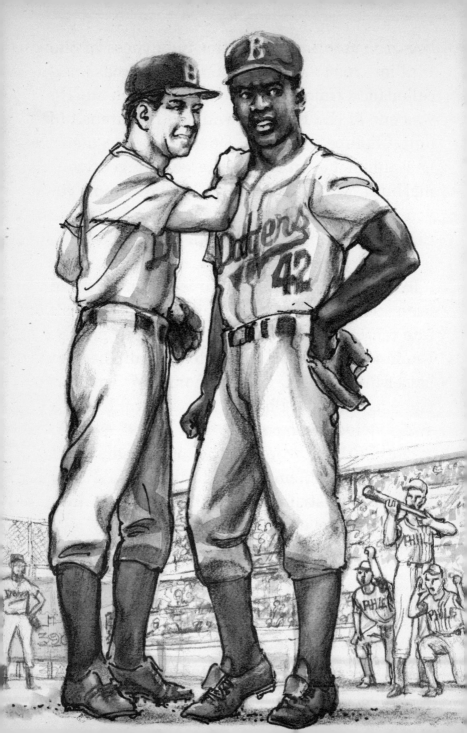

getting threatening letters. Some crazy person threatened to hurt Rae, kidnap our baby and to murder me if I didn't get out of baseball right away. We had to play Philadelphia again, and I couldn't stop thinking about those threats. The Phillies must have heard about the threats because they aimed their bats at me as if they were guns and made shooting noises. I was very upset about all of this, but I think now that it was a blessing in disguise. Pee Wee Reese called time out. He came over to me and put his arm around my shoulders just to show everyone that he was with me all the way.

The rest of the Dodgers also began to come to my defense. But it wasn't enough. The pressure to take all of these insults and threats and not fight back was beginning to get to me. I began to make some mistakes playing first base, and my hitting got worse. People told Branch to bench me, but he was giving me time to loosen up.

Every time I got up to bat, pitchers would deliberately try to hit me and aim for my head. I got hit by the ball six times in the opening weeks of the season.

I started to get angry. By the time we came up against the Phillies again I was angry enough to show them that I was a baseball player they had to watch out for. In the fourth inning, I got on first base. The four players behind me finished what I had started and each got a hit. That put us ahead three to two. In the sixth inning I made it to first base again. Pee Wee Reese was on third. I drove the pitcher crazy with my attempts to steal second base. In his desire to get me out, he let Pee Wee slip by and steal home. In the eighth inning, with two men out, I hit a home run.

We won that game, and many games after that. I really began hitting the ball; I had hits in twenty one straight games. I stole so many bases that the players were encouraged by my will to win. We moved into first place in the league, and stayed there. By the end of the season, I was named "Rookie of the Year." I had captured the hearts of the Brooklyn fans. People mobbed me wherever I went, asking for autographs—especially the kids. On September

23, the people of Brooklyn declared a "Jackie Robinson Day" and gave me many gifts, including a new car. But the best gift of all came without any applause. A new pitcher was signed to play on the Dodgers. His name was Dan Bankhead, and he was black.

The next year the Dodgers signed three more black players. The owners of the other teams were starting to think that they should also bring in some black players. I made it my personal crusade to try to persuade all the owners to sign blacks. The toughest man to convince was the owner of the Yankees.

Meanwhile, I still had to put up with all those insults and wild pitches. Even though more blacks were in the major leagues, our position was not secure. I began to get sick from the effort of keeping all my anger bottled up inside of me. Finally, in 1949, Rickey told me that I could behave to all the bullies who had been taunting me for so long, any way I wanted. The "noble experiment" was over. Black players had become an official part of major league baseball. We were here to stay. One by one, I went up to those bullies. Once they saw that I would not just take it, they backed away in a hurry.

I switched from first base to second base. Pee

Wee Reese, the shortstop and my closest friend on the team, and I became known for our lightning-fast double plays. It was as if each of us knew by instinct what the other would do in any situation.

We kept winning games and ultimately, league championships. We couldn't seem to win the World Series, though. Year after year, we would lose to the New York Yankees. I didn't want to retire until we had beaten the Yankees. I was still angry at the owner for not hiring a black player.

I was getting old, though. My body had been through a lot of wear and tear. I was also getting old from all those years of taking the insults and threats. I was losing my speed. I tried to use my mind more, and become a thinking player rather than an athletic player. I began really studying each batter who came up to the plate, so that I could pick the best place to stand.

I knew that retirement was just around the corner, but we had to beat those Yankees first. The Yankees were a great team, but no better than we were. They felt at home being the World Champions, while we were used to *almost* winning. Our fans were the most loyal, though. They called us the "Beloved Bums," and their battle cry was "Wait till next year!" I knew we had to *think* we could win before we could win.

In 1955, we were playing the Yankees again for the World Championship. It was the eighth inning of the first game and we were behind by a score of six to three. I looked around the dugout, and I saw that my teammates felt that the series was already over, and that the Yankees would win again. They thought the Yankees had jinxed us.

I decided that we were not going to lose this time, not if I could help it. "Let's go Carl!" I yelled to the Dodger who was stepping up to bat.

I could tell he had heard me. He hit a single. The next player also hit the ball, but it was caught. Then I was up. I hit the ball and sent Carl to third base while I ran to first and then second. The next batter drove Carl home. We were now behind by a score of six to four. I was on third base.

When I was younger, I might have had a chance to steal home against the mighty New York Yankees, but now? I just knew that I had to do something. I had to let the other Dodgers know that the Yankees hadn't jinxed us.

The Yankee pitcher, Whitey Ford, saw me taking a lead off third base, and only grinned at me.

I must have seemed like just an old man, wasting time trying to get him rattled. As soon as he went into his wind-up, I was off. He threw his fastest speedball to his catcher, Yogi Berra, but it was too late. I was home safe. We lost that game and the one after that. In the third game, though, I started my old base-running tricks. The Yankee pitcher became so rattled that we loaded the bases on walks and scored twice. We beat them by a score of eight to three. Then we won the fourth game. The series was tied at two games apiece. We didn't feel jinxed anymore, but the Yankees didn't give up easily. They won the fifth game, but we took the final two. We were Champions!

At the end of the baseball season in 1956, I retired. I wasn't forgotten though. My uniform number, forty-two, was also retired—never to be worn by any other Dodger. In 1962, I was voted into the Baseball Hall of Fame, the first among many black players who were to follow.

I didn't stop trying to knock down that wall between white and black Americans after I stopped playing baseball, though. I helped to start a bank to lend black people money to start their own businesses. I worked with young blacks to teach them self-respect. I advised a New York Governor on Civil Rights and wrote about them in a newspaper column. I also gave my time and support to Martin Luther King, Jr. to help him in his own fight to knock down the wall. He even presented me a Honorary Degree from Howard University for speaking out against racism.

There were, and still are, more ways than one to break down that wall, and I wanted to try all of them in my lifetime. Although I didn't manage to knock the wall down completely, it is much less solid than it was before. What remains of the wall still needs to be destroyed in order for white people and black people to live together in peace.

Now that you have finished reading this book, you have learned about one man's fight against racism. As it says in the Declaration of Independence, "We hold these truths to be self evident, that all men are created equal, that they are endowed by their creator with certain inalienable Rights, that among these are Life, Liberty and the pursuit of Happiness." Now, it is your turn to help rid the world of prejudice.

The Life and Times of
Jackie Robinson

1919   Jack Roosevelt Robinson is born in Georgia on January 31.

1936   Jackie's older brother, Mack, wins a silver medal in the two-hundred meter dash at the Olympics in Germany. The black American athlete Jesse Owens wins four gold medals.

1938   Jackie sets the American Junior College broad jumping record. He also becomes known as a football, basketball and baseball star.

1939   Jackie goes to UCLA and wins varsity letters in four sports—the first four-letter athlete in UCLA history.

1941   The Japanese bomb Pearl Harbor, on December 7. America enters World War II.

1942   Jackie joins the army. He fights for his right to go to Officers Candidates School.

1943   Jackie is made a second lieutenant and fights for the rights of other black servicemen at the army base.

Jackie has to stand trial on an unjust charge because he refused to take a back seat on a bus. He is found innocent of the charges, but loses his chance to go overseas to fight with the troops he trained.

1945   After leaving the army, Jackie plays for an all-black baseball team, the Kansas City Monarchs. Jackie meets Branch Rickey and is hired to play for the Montreal Royals.

1946   Jackie electrifies fans with his playing style and leads the Royals to the Minor League World Championship in the Little World Series.

1947   Jackie joins the Brooklyn Dodgers on April 15. He becomes the first black man to play in the major leagues. In spite of threats to his life, he wins the coveted "Rookie of the Year" award. Brooklyn fans declare a "Jackie Robinson Day."

1948   More black players are signed by the Dodgers. Other teams begin to consider doing the same.

1955   The Dodgers win the World Series, finally beating the Yankees.

1956   Jackie retires from baseball, but continues to fight racism.

1962   Jackie is inducted into the Baseball Hall of Fame in Cooperstown, New York.

1972   Jackie dies on October 24.